# Gratitude

# Gratitude

Dani DiPirro

WATKINS
Sharing Wisdom Since
1893

**Gratitude**

Dani DiPirro

First published in the UK and USA in 2016
by Watkins, an imprint of Watkins
Media Limited
19 Cecil Court
London WC2N 4EZ

enquiries@watkinspublishing.co.uk

Development Editor: Kelly Thompson
Senior Editor: Fiona Robertson
Editor: Dawn Bates
Design Manager: Viki Ottewill
Design: Dani DiPirro
Production: Uzma Taj

A CIP record for this book is available
from the British Library

ISBN: 978-1-78028-931-1

10 9 8 7 6 5 4 3 2 1

Typeset in Gotham
Printed in China

www.watkinspublishing.com

To anyone who has inspired me to be grateful, thank you. You are the reason I was able to connect with gratitude and create this book.

# INTRODUCTION

Gratitude is a powerful force. New research suggests that gratitude not only creates psychological wellbeing but even improves *physical* health. When you're focused on what you're thankful for, it's difficult to feel negative or unhappy, making the cultivation of gratitude one of the best ways to live a happy, fulfilled life.

Of course, life does have its downs as well as its ups, and when you're navigating a particularly stormy patch, paying attention to what you have (instead of what you lack) can be really hard work.

This little book has been designed to help you embrace an attitude of gratitude – even when it might seem like it's a challenge to do so. Pairing inspiring quotes with fresh insights and motivating activities, this book will set you on the path to a more thankful, more joyful life.

# GRATITUDE

noun | grat•i•tude

1. The quality or feeling of being warmly or deeply appreciative of kindness or benefits received

2. The state of being grateful or appreciative

He is a **wise man** who does not grieve for the things which he has not, but **rejoices for those which he has.**

Epictetus
Greek philosopher (AD 55–135)

It is all too easy to crave things you don't have, especially when you see others enjoying them, but true wisdom comes from appreciating what is already yours. Instead of wanting what you can't have, you can simply choose to be thankful and focus on what is within you and around you.

*Make a point to begin each day by stating three things for which you are thankful.*

TODAY I AM
GRATEFUL
FOR WHAT
I HAVE
**RIGHT
NOW.**

> **Let us be grateful to people who make us happy; they are the charming gardeners who make our souls blossom.**

Marcel Proust
French novelist (1871–1922)

Treasure the people in your life who make you feel good about yourself. They have encouraged you to grow into the person you are today, and they will support you in developing further. Not everyone will make you feel great but you can choose to surround yourself with those who do.

*Contact three people and tell them how grateful you are for them.*

# TODAY I AM THANKFUL FOR **OTHERS' SUPPORT.**

**Keep your eyes open to your mercies** . . . the man who forgets to be **grateful** has **fallen asleep** in life.

Robert Louis Stevenson
Scottish writer (1850–1894)

SLOW DOWN ♦♦♦
♦♦♦ **AWAKEN** ♦♦♦
APPRECIATE ♦♦♦♦

It is all too easy to charge through life, focused on the next task on your to-do list. To fully embrace all life has to offer, try staying alert to the compassion others send your way. Recognize the situations in which you experience life's little mercies, such as kindness and forgiveness.

*Reflect on the last time you experienced compassion or forgiveness.*

TODAY I
AM AWARE
OF **SMALL
BLESSINGS.**

**Gratitude is the memory of the heart.**

Jean Massieu
French deaf educator (1772–1846)

GRATITUDE ◆◆◆◆
◆◆◆◆◆◆◆ **MEMORY**
HEART ◆◆◆◆◆◆◆◆

One of the mind's most amazing abilities is its power to hold on to memories. Consider how beautiful it is to be capable of summoning up a time when you felt loved and connected, dispelling feelings of sadness you might have in the present. Call upon and be thankful for those precious memories.

*Write down one memory you are truly thankful to have within your heart.*

# TODAY I AM THANKFUL FOR **FOND MEMORIES.**

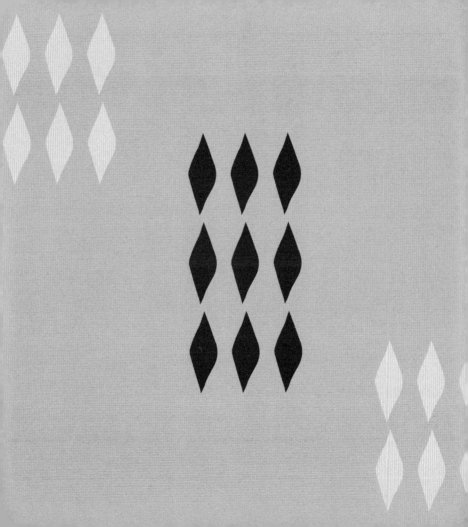

**Gratitude bestows reverence,** allowing us to encounter **everyday epiphanies** . . . that change forever how we experience **life.**

John Milton
English poet (1608–1674)

AMAZING ◆◆◆◆◆◆
**LIFE-CHANGING**
◆AWE-INSPIRING

Look around you and admire and appreciate everything in your world. As you find wonderment in small, everyday experiences, your life will become more joyful and you will feel more content. What may have seemed mundane yesterday will feel magical today.

*Find wonder in something you experience today.*

TODAY I AM
GRATEFUL FOR
**EVERYDAY
MAGIC.**

**Some people grumble** that roses have thorns; I am grateful that **thorns have roses**.

Alphonse Karr
French writer (1808–1890)

ROSES ◆◆◆◆◆◆◆◆

◆◆ **GRATITUDE** ◆◆

◆◆◆◆◆◆◆◆ BEAUTY

Your "inner voice" may tend to focus on the negative, and it can take time and practice to silence that. To help quiet this negative voice, seek out what inspires gratitude. Try looking for the positive and sharing it with others to reinforce this perspective in your own mind.

*The next time you notice a thorn in your life, seek out the rose.*

# TODAY I WILL APPRECIATE THE GOOD IN LIFE.

**Gratitude is a currency** that we can mint for ourselves and **spend without fear** of bankruptcy.

Fred De Witt Van Amburgh
American writer (1866–1944)

Thankfulness is something that is available to us all, every day, whatever our circumstances. You might want to appreciate silently all that you have, or perhaps make someone else's day by thanking them openly. Use the currency of gratitude whenever you can, and the rewards will soon come to you.

*Say thank you to someone in each situation you find yourself today.*

TODAY I AM
HAPPY THAT
**"THANKS"
IS FREE.**

The **essence** of all **beautiful art**, all great art, is **gratitude**.

Friedrich Nietzsche
German philosopher (1844–1900)

◆◆◆◆ CREATE ◆◆◆◆
◆◆◆◆ **CAPTIVATE**
CHERISH ◆◆◆◆◆◆

A sense of beauty comes from a place of appreciation. When you are open to the wonder of life (in both the good and the bad things that happen), you can draw on gratitude to recognize beauty and even create it yourself. Being creative is a way of saying "thanks" for all you have in life.

*Create a thing of beauty: a conversation, a piece of art, a good meal.*

# TODAY I AM THANKFUL FOR THE ABILITY TO CREATE.

"Gratitude can transform **common days into thanksgivings** . . . and change ordinary **opportunities into blessings**.

William Arthur Ward
American writer (1921–1994)

◆◆◆◆ TRANSFORM
◆◆ **BLESSINGS** ◆◆
JOY ◆◆◆◆◆◆◆◆◆◆

Even a routine job can become joyful if you choose to open your heart to gratitude. If you resent domestic chores, can you be glad that you have a home to clean? If you dislike your job, can you be thankful for the good health that enables you to work and for the chance to bond with others?

*Today, make use of one of your unique abilities or talents.*

TODAY I AM FINDING **NEW WAYS** TO BE GRATEFUL.

**Thankfulness may consist merely of words. Gratitude is shown in acts.**

Henri-Frédéric Amiel
Swiss philosopher (1821–1881)

ACTION ◆◆◆◆◆◆◆◆
**THANKFULNESS**
◆◆◆◆◆◆◆◆◆ SHOW

Saying "thank you" is a polite habit most people acquire at an early age, but really conveying your gratitude to someone requires more thought and effort. Can you show how you feel? Take the time to think of acts that communicate your thanks – they will be remembered and appreciated.

*Complete one kind, thankful act for a loved one.*

TODAY I AM
**GLAD** TO
SHOW MY
THANKS.

"

I have learned . . . to be almost **unconsciously grateful – as a child is** – for a sunny day, blue water, flowers in a vase

"

Faith Baldwin
American author (1893–1978)

WONDER ◆◆◆◆◆◆◆
◆◆**CHILDLIKE** ◆◆
◆◆◆◆◆◆◆◆◆◆◆◆◆ AWE

As adults, we are often too busy to appreciate what is around us. Even when you are at your most frantic, try pausing for a moment and just looking. You are sure to spot something that surprises you! In this way, you can recapture some of the positivity and awestruck wonder you had as a child.

*Look carefully at the world around you, as if from a child's point of view.*

# TODAY I AM GRATEFUL FOR THE CHILD IN ME.

> **The thankful heart** . . . will find, in every hour, some **heavenly blessings.**

Henry Ward Beecher
American clergyman (1813–1887)

NOTICE ◆◆◆◆◆◆◆◆
◆◆ **BLESSINGS** ◆◆
◆◆◆◆◆◆◆◆◆ ALWAYS

It is often easier to complain and be negative than to be cheery and positive. This may be habitual behaviour or simply a way of making conversation. For a happier and more contented life, set yourself the task of literally counting your blessings every night before you go to sleep.

Today, *every hour*, *write down* one thing that makes you feel thankful.

TODAY I AM
APPRECIATIVE
OF **EVERY
HOUR**
OF THE
DAY.

**Joy** is the simplest
form of **gratitude**.

Karl Barth
Swiss theologian (1886–1968)

◆◆◆◆◆◆◆◆◆◆◆ JOY
**UNCOMPLICATED**
◆◆◆◆◆ PURE ◆◆◆◆◆

Pure joy is gratitude rising from the heart, sometimes in response to good news, and at other times simply as a flood of thankfulness for everyday blessings. We can't anticipate these moments of joyful consciousness, but we can open our hearts to them, and cherish them when they happen.

*Recognize your gratitude the next time you experience pure joy.*

TODAY I AM THANKFUL FOR **JOYFUL MOMENTS.**

# Everything has **beauty** but **not everyone sees** it.

**Confucius**
**Chinese philosopher (551–479 BC)**

The world can sometimes seem an ugly place, so it is down to us to actively seek out the beauty. As much of life's experience depends on our own perceptions, feelings and expectations, try cultivating an inner spirit of thankfulness, and you will be amazed how much more beauty you can see.

*Find beauty in something today and show it to someone else.*

TODAY I AM
HAPPY TO
**SHARE LIFE'S
BEAUTY.**

**Two kinds** of gratitude: the sudden kind we feel for what we take; **the larger kind we feel for what we give.**

Edwin Arlington Robinson
American poet (1869–1935)

GIVE ◆◆◆◆◆◆◆◆◆◆◆◆◆
◆◆◆◆◆ **FEEL** ◆◆◆◆◆
◆◆◆◆ FULFILMENT

True thankfulness can be felt when you donate your time, your energy or your possessions to someone in need. Being able to give to others is a privilege because it means we have something that will make someone's life better – and that is a profound source of gratitude.

*Donate a possession to someone in need.*

TODAY I AM
GRATEFUL
FOR THE
**ABILITY
TO GIVE.**

**Courtesies of a small and trivial character** are the ones which **strike deepest** in the grateful and appreciating heart.

Henry Clay
American politician (1777–1852)

COURTESY ◆◆◆◆ ◆◆◆◆
◆◆◆◆ **HEART** ◆◆◆◆ ◆◆◆◆
◆◆◆◆◆◆ APPRECIATE

True courtesy is often about finding a subtle but heartfelt way of expressing thanks, rather than necessarily making a grand gesture. A small handmade gift can mean more than a shop-bought item; a quick phone call at the right moment says more than a fancy bouquet of flowers.

*Commit an act of kindness – smile at a stranger or hold a door open for someone.*

TODAY I AM
GLAD TO BE
**KIND IN
SMALL
WAYS.**

66

A **grateful mind** is
a great mind which
eventually **attracts**
**to itself great things.**

Plato
Greek philosopher (428–348 BC)

# GRATEFUL ◆◆◆◆◆◆◆
◆◆◆◆◆ **MIND** ◆◆◆◆◆
◆◆◆◆ATTRACTION

Like attracts like, so the more you focus on being grateful, the more thank-worthy things (and people) you will have in your life. Being thankful releases you from a focus on negativity, opening the way to achieving greater things in life. And along the way, you will be an inspiration to others, too!

*When tempted to complain, list good things you are lucky to possess.*

TODAY I AM
THANKFUL
FOR MY
**GRATEFUL
MIND.**

# Gratitude is not only the greatest of **virtues** but the **parent** of all others.

Marcus Tullius Cicero
Roman philosopher (107–43 BC)

When you are thankful, you cultivate a good-hearted nature that influences all aspects of your inner self. Start by being grateful, and then watch as other virtues such as love, kindness, patience and honour follow. Day by day you will become happier and feel more fulfilled in your life.

*Identify one virtue you possess that is strengthened by gratitude.*

TODAY I AM
GRATEFUL
FOR **ALL MY
VIRTUES.**

# TOP 10 WAYS TO EXPERIENCE GRATITUDE

1. Value what you already have.

2. Overlook what you lack.

3. Choose thankful over wishful.

4. Appreciate the little things.

5. Savour moments spent alone.

6. Give words of thanks to others.

7. Recognize your strengths.

8. Treasure your relationships.

9. Cherish your inspiration.

10. Welcome whatever comes.

# TOP 10 WAYS TO BE GRATEFUL AT WORK

1. Appreciate having a purpose.

2. Look for the good in your colleagues.

3. Be thankful for the skills you have.

4. Appreciate the technology you use.

5. Welcome routine and certainty.

6. Help out a new co-worker.

7. Enjoy a work-free lunchtime.

8. Choose to be positive.

9. Learn from your boss and others.

10. Imagine life without an income.

# TOP 10 WAYS TO BE THANKFUL AT HOME

1. Look around and appreciate it all!

2. Turn off your phone and be at peace.

3. Invite others to enjoy your home.

4. Be thankful for your loved ones.

5. Open the window and look out.

6. Appreciate pets that bring you joy.

7. Try a different seat for a new outlook.

8. Go for a walk in your neighbourhood.

9. Keep things you value in good order.

10. Treat your loved ones to healthy food.

# TOP 10 WAYS TO APPRECIATE A TOUGH DAY

1. Get perspective by talking to a friend.

2. Learn from the challenges you faced.

3. List what was *good* about today.

4. Allow yourself to feel what you feel.

5. Do something to de-stress.

6. Reward yourself with a favourite meal.

7. Download a book or a film as a treat.

8. Do something nice for someone else.

9. Praise yourself for surviving the day.

10. Accept today and look to tomorrow.

# TOP 10 WAYS TO BE GRATEFUL FOR YOURSELF

1. Be thankful for your best qualities.

2. Give of yourself by being a friend.

3. Appreciate your health and wealth.

4. Teach someone else one of your skills.

5. Recall a compliment you received.

6. Notice how well your body works.

7. Smile at yourself in the mirror (daily!).

8. Use your talents to be creative.

9. See mistakes as a way to learn.

10. Be kind and loving to yourself.

# NOTE TO READER

**Hello!** I'm Dani. I hope you've enjoyed reading this little book as much as I enjoyed creating it. Gratitude is such an important part of my life, and it is essential for what I strive to do on a daily basis: stay positive and stay present.

In 2009 I created **PositivelyPresent.com**. Since setting up that website, I've gone on to write multiple ebooks and publish *The Positively Present Guide to Life*, as well as design diaries for Watkins' *Every Day Matters* series. I also work as a graphic designer. I am so grateful to have so much in my life – and even more thankful that I'm able to share my insights about the power of gratitude with you in this book!

If you want to learn more about me or my work, check out **DaniDiPirro.com**, or visit **PositivelyPresent.com** for inspiration on living positively in the present.